Where's Stitch? A Search-And-Find Activity Book

Story: Daniele Mittica for Arancia Studio
Text: Silvia Dell'Amore
Pencils: Elisa Pocetta for Arancia Studio
Paints: Silvia Bancora, Arianna Stefani for Arancia Studio
Design: Mauro Abbattista
Cover design: Alessandro Susin
Production: Giulia Caparrelli
© 2024 Disney

First published in the UK in 2024 by Studio Press, an imprint of Bonnier Books UK,
4th Floor, Victoria House, Bloomsbury Square, London WC1B 4DA

Owned by Bonnier Books,
Sveavägen 56, Stockholm, Sweden
www.bonnierbooks.co.uk

Printed in Latvia
9 10

ISBN 978-1-83587-026-6

MIX
Paper | Supporting
responsible forestry
FSC
www.fsc.org
FSC® C002795

STITCH IS RIDING TO THE RESCUE!

Everything is going great in Kauaʻi, until one day . . . the sea waves disappear!

The surfers are sad because there are no waves to ride.

But Stitch has a plan. He wants to build a machine to make

the perfect sea waves – but first, he needs some special parts.

So he goes on a space adventure!

Will Stitch manage to help his friends and bring back the waves?

Before we find out, let's meet the characters – there is at least one

to find in every scene!

Stitch

Once upon a time, there was an alien known as 'Experiment 626'. But now everyone knows him as Stitch, Lilo's funny pet! He lives with Lilo and her sister, Nani, on the island of Kauaʻi. They're like his ʻohana, his family, and love him loads – even when he's up to mischief!

Lilo

Don't be fooled by her young age – Lilo sure knows how to speak her mind! Young and smart, Lilo adores dancing, grooving to rock'n'roll songs and, of course, sharing tons of giggles and silly adventures with her best friend, Stitch!

Nani

Nani is Lilo's sweet and loving big sister and acts as a motherly figure for her. Taking care of Lilo and Stitch is Nani's daily mission. Even when things get a little tricky, Nani works extra hard to ensure they're both feeling loved and super happy!

David

David isn't just an excellent surfer – he's an awesome friend, too! He's always there for Nani when she needs someone to talk to. When he's not riding the waves, David can often be found hanging out with Nani and her 'ohana.

Myrtle

Myrtle is Lilo's age, and they even go to the same hula (the traditional dance of Hawai'i) class, but other than that, they don't seem to have much in common. She can be a bit spoiled and bossy sometimes, but Lilo knows just how to handle her.

Cobra Bubbles

Cobra Bubbles is a very serious social worker who cares a lot about children. When he first meets Lilo and Nani, he's a bit confused by their messy life, but he quickly figures out they really need each other.

Jumba

Jumba is a super-smart scientist who loves doing experiments, and one of his creations is Experiment 626! He can be a bit self-assured, but deep down, he's got a good and kind side – especially when it comes to little Lilo!

Pleakley

Pleakley is a funny one-eyed alien who thinks he knows everything about Earth ... or does he? The moment he lands on the planet, he realizes his knowledge is a little mixed-up. Maybe spending more time on Earth will help him get it right!

The Grand Councilwoman

The Grand Councilwoman is the no-nonsense leader of the United Galactic Federation. Even though she can be really firm and strict, she knows how to be fair, especially when it means keeping a new ʻohana united and happy!

Captain Gantu

Captain Gantu is a tough and quick-tempered alien who used to work for the United Galactic Federation. As a soldier, he's very impressive, but Experiment 626 always manages to outsmart him!

The Beach

It's just another bright day on the beautiful island of Kaua'i!
The sun is shining, the sand feels warm and cosy and the waves . . .
Wait, where are the waves? The sea is strangely still!
While David and the other surfers wonder what's going on,
see if you can spot Stitch amid the beach crowd!

Lilo's School

Stitch can't wait to investigate the mystery of the missing waves, but first, he has to join Lilo for something special. It's Take Your Pet to School Day! The classroom is bursting with fluffy friends, and Stitch is doing his best to stay out of trouble . . . well, sort of! Can you find him in the midst of all this adorable chaos?

Halloween Street Party

It's night time, and the waves are still missing . . . but Stitch's detective plans will have to wait because it's Halloween, and he's ready for some fun! Stitch just loves to play tricks on Halloween, especially when Nani is not around to tell him off! Can you see him among all of those cool costumes?

SWEET HAWAII

Under the Sea

Since they can't find the waves, Lilo, Nani and their friends decide to have an underwater adventure instead. They dive into the sea to explore all the colourful creatures! Lilo's got her peanut butter sandwiches ready for her fish friends. And where is Stitch? See if it's easier to spot him underwater!

The Outdoor Market

Stitch is determined to build a machine to bring back the waves. But first, he must find the parts he needs to make it. He starts his search at the outdoor market. The stalls are filled with colourful fruits and objects. Will he find what he needs? And will you find him in the lively crowd?

Landing Site

The United Galactic Federation is gearing up to leave planet Earth when suddenly Stitch appears out of nowhere. He thinks he will find what he needs in space and wants to sneak aboard the ship! Are you up for the challenge of spotting him among all those busy aliens?

The Spaceship Command Deck

Bye-bye, Kaua'i! While all kinds of aliens are buzzing around, Stitch is hunting for the parts he needs for his waves machine. But before he gets back to work, he can't resist checking out the command deck with all its awesome buttons!
Can you spot him having fun?

19

The Spaceship Cafeteria

It's lunchtime on the spaceship, and all the aliens rush
to the cafeteria for some yummy treats and a well-deserved break.
Meanwhile, Stitch is still on his mission to fix the waves, but
those space noodles, muffins, and burgers sure look tempting. . . .
He must be nearby! Can you see him?

The Galactic Federation

Still no luck finding a solution for the waves . . . but maybe Stitch will discover something useful in the big hall where the Galactic Federation meets! It's a huge room packed with alien delegates of all shapes and sizes. Can you spot Stitch among all those wiggly tentacles and funny eyes?

Open Space

Stitch has finally found something useful, so it's time to blast back to Earth! He hops aboard a tiny spaceship and prepares for an epic space journey. Next stop: Kaua'i! But he'd better watch out for all the weird and wacky spaceships and objects floating around. Can you spot Stitch zooming away?

Jumba's Laboratory

Now Stitch has to take all the cool stuff he found in space to Jumba. His lab is not far from Lilo and Nani's house, but . . . uh-oh, it's a total mess! It's packed with tons of weird things and spare parts everywhere! Do you think Stitch can find Jumba in all that chaos? And even more importantly, can you see Stitch?

The Great Wave

Thanks to all the awesome stuff Stitch found, Jumba built
a fantastic machine that makes the perfect waves for surfing.
It works like magic! Now David and all the surfers can catch
the most epic waves ever. Of course, Lilo and the whole 'ohana join
in the fun . . . but where's Stitch? Can you spot him?

Lū'au

To celebrate the waves coming back, Lilo and her friends decide to throw a big party. They're having a Lū'au, a super-fun Hawaiian festival! The beach is packed with hula dancers, yummy food, and everyone is having a great time. Especially Stitch, who is . . . wait, where is he? Can you find him enjoying the party somewhere?

FIND ALL THE HIDDEN TARGETS

The Beach

 This bag

 This alien

 Pleakley

 This ball

 David

Lilo's School

 This eraser

 This parrot

 This pencil

 This dog

 This lizard

Halloween Street Party

 Captain Gantu

 This pumpkin

 This kid

 This apple

 This alien

Remember, 'ohana means nobody gets left behind! Let's go back to each location and hunt for all the hidden characters and objects listed below and in the next pages. Can you find them all?

Under the Sea

 This fish

 Jumba

 Lilo

 This seahorse

 Nani

The Outdoor Market

 Myrtle

 This dog

 This pink flower

 This woman

 This ice cream

Landing Site

 This Federation member

 This butterfly

 This pair of pliers

 This plant

 Cobra Bubbles

The Spaceship Command Deck

 This joystick

 These glasses

 This alien

 This sandwich

 This notebook

The Spaceship Cafeteria

 This alien

 This robot

 This red bowl

 This spoon

 This salt shaker

The Galactic Federation

 This alien

 This robot

 Grand Councilwoman

 This robot

 This alien

Open Space

 This spaceship

 This flying robot

 This alien

 This puppy robot

 Gantu's spaceship

Jumba's Laboratory

 This clock

 This hair dryer

 This microscope

 This cable

 This boot

The Great Wave

 This boy

 This dog

 This singer

 This blue paddle

 This pink surfboard

Lū 'au

 This pink bowl

 This woman

 This pillow

 This girl

 This pineapple

SOLUTIONS

Ta-da! Stitch is circled in red, hidden target characters and objects

are circled in white, and other characters are circled in blue.

How did you do? Whether you found them all or not,

your 'ohana is proud of you!

The Beach

Lilo's School

Halloween
Street Party

Under the
Sea

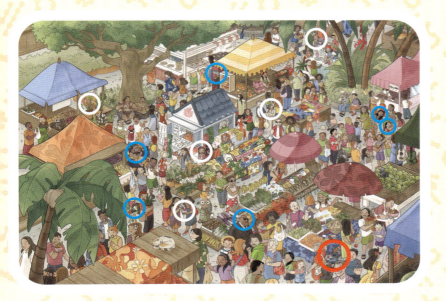

The Outdoor
Market

Landing Site

The Spaceship Command Deck

The Spaceship Cafeteria

The Galactic Federation

Open Space

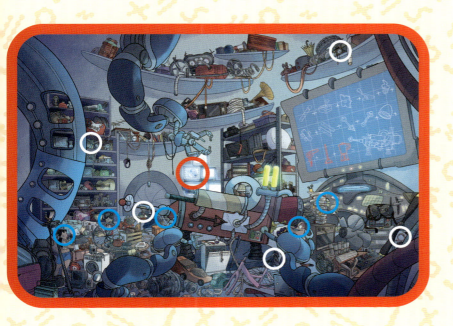

Jumba's Laboratory

The Great Wave

Lū ʻau